PAPER

BOY

Paper Boy

David Huddle

UNIVERSITY OF PITTSBURGH PRESS

Published by the University of Pittsburgh Press, Pittsburgh, Pa., 15260
Copyright © 1979, David Huddle
All rights reserved
Feffer and Simons, Inc., London
Manufactured in the United States of America

Library of Congress Cataloging in Publication Data

Huddle, David, 1942–
  Paper boy.

  (Pitt poetry series)
  I. Title.
PS3558.U287P3   811'.5'4   78-23232
ISBN 0-8229-3392-6
ISBN 0-8229-5302-1 pbk.

Grateful acknowledgment is made to the editors of the journals in which some
of these poems first appeared: *Dark Horse, Harper's, The Richmond Broom.*
"Gregory's House," "Miss Florence Jackson," "Jeep Alley, Emperor of Base-
ball," and "My Brother Flies Over Low," © 1977 by *Jam To-Day*, are re-
printed by permission from issue no. 5. "Mrs Green" was first published in
Esquire.

The publication of this book is supported by a grant from the National Endowment for the Arts in Washington, D.C., a Federal agency.

for my grandfather
Charles Ross Huddle
1885–1970

CONTENTS

These poems are fictions.
The truth they attempt to achieve
is personal and imaginative, not historical.

PAPER

BOY

TOWN HISTORY, 1917

J. C. Lawson,
my great-grandfather,
came there poor,
built up a livery
stable, a funeral
parlor, a watch repair
shop, and a general
store. In 1917,
when my daddy had sat
in his lap all morning,
my great-grandfather
walked outside,
got shot, and died
that afternoon.
A posse was sent
from Wytheville,
but they didn't catch
Fred Hill until he
gave himself up
the next morning.
My daddy was 7
at the time, and Aunt
Elrica, in her teens,
went into shock
and clasped her hand
over my daddy's mouth
to stop his crying.
She almost smothered
him before he could
get her hand pried
loose.

HOLES COMMENCE FALLING

The lead & zinc company
owned the mineral rights
to the whole town anyway,
and after drilling holes
for 3 or 4 years,
they finally found the right
place and sunk a mine shaft.
We were proud
of all that digging,
even though nobody from
town got hired. They
were going to dig right
under New River and hook up
with the mine at Austinville.
Then people's wells
started drying up just like
somebody'd shut off a faucet,
and holes commenced falling,
big chunks of people's yards
would drop 5 or 6 feet,
houses would shift and crack.
Now and then the company'd
pay out a little money
in damages; they got a truck
to haul water and sell it
to the people whose wells
had dried up, but most
everbody agreed the
situation wasn't
serious.

MY DADDY,
WHENEVER HE WENT SOME PLACE

Brought gifts
home for me
and my brother
until once the bag
from the 5 & 10
had hammers in it,
which my brother
liked just fine,
took his out
to the back porch
steps, started
driving nails
right away, but
which for some
reason nobody
understands, me
least of all,
offended me,
made me cry
a long time,
and it didn't
take us long
to get used
to the fact
that after that
whenever he
went some place
my daddy was
damn sure
coming back
empty-handed.

ALMOST GOING

Uncle Bill had been there
and said it had
a lovely climate,
so my father applied
for a high-paying job
at a mine in Cyprus.
He and my mother talked
to my brother and me
about it, let us stay
up past our bedtimes.
For several weeks
the house was full
of sunlight, and we
laughed about everything,
but a letter came
turning him down,
and we were relieved,
Mother saying we had
no business in Cyprus
anyway, because she'd
grown up right
in that same house
where we lived,
had married my father
when she was 15,
and he'd grown up
over at Grandmama's
across the field.
We took family trips
to Williamsburg,
Washington, D.C.,
and our favorite one
of all, the Great
Smoky Mountains.

DELIVERING THE TIMES, 1952–1955

80 papers
was all there was
in the whole town,
a 4-mile walk
before school
and 3 dogs
I had to watch out for.
Crow Jim King
broke me in.
He showed me
how to blow snot
out of one side
of my nose holding
the other side shut
with my finger.
In 2 years
I saved $90,
sent off to a Roanoke
pawn shop
for that gold-plated
trumpet Daddy
had to teach me how
to play. And even
though Sunday
was a heavy load,
I walked that route
every day until
I had to start
catching the bus
to the consolidated
high school.

GREGORY'S HOUSE

It was a testimony
to something that
could make my daddy
mad even talking about
it, how when one side
of the house collapsed
they just stopped using
those rooms, and when
the front porch dropped
off Gregory was upset
because he had to do
his drinking in the
kitchen with the kids
whining all around him
and the TV turned up so
loud he couldn't half
concentrate. And they
say when the outhouse
folded over one January
Gregory cut a hole in
the floor and was happy
not to have to make that
trip in cold weather.
But every Saturday
morning they sent out
one dirty-fisted child
to pay me for the paper.
Until that Sunday I
threw a heavy, rolled-up
one too high and up onto

the roof, and it fell
right on through, and
the next Saturday Gregory
himself came out to the
fence and cussed me and
said I owed him damages
for knocking a hole in
his house.

DROWNING

Twin brothers drowned
when I was in fifth grade.
I don't remember who it was
came up the hill to tell us,
but we walked down there
to watch the rescue squad
in boats out dragging
the water with ropes and hooks.
By that time two or three
hundred people were there
beside the river,
clustered and talking.
There had been four of them:
Pete Bushey, Pig Clemons,
and Joe and Charles.
Pete and Pig had made it
to the banks all right,
but the other two, the twins,
were still in the water,
and Joe and Charles always
wore high-top shoes.
They'd broken a lock to get
somebody's old flat-bottomed boat
out to where the current was strong,
and then it had turned over
and sunk on them.
I watched them pull one
and then the other up
out of the brown water
and into the boats.
They had on blue shirts, just alike.

My mother went over
to where the men brought them in
to ask if they were sure
nothing could be done
to make them live.
I could hear her voice,
too high,
even over where I stood
with my daddy and my brother.
But they were dead sure enough,
and we walked back
in the hot June afternoon,
my mother stubbing her toe
on a railroad tie
and hurting it bad.

FUNERAL

We went to the house
to see Joe and Charles.
In the living room
behind the white scrim
they looked magical
and still.
Thelma cried
when Mother took me in
the bedroom to see her.
She hugged me too tight.
I wanted to go back and
look at my friends again.
In the Church of God
my whole fifth grade class
sat in a row up front,
and none of us cried
even though there were people
crying all around us.
When they finished singing
they had all the classmates
line up on the steps,
stand there and hold flowers
while they brought out
the shut caskets.
When they had let them down,
we lined up
and threw handfuls of dirt
down on the tops.
I went home and practiced
my recital piece on the piano.

I felt bad a long time
that summer, but then later on
I fell off the roof
and cut my head,
and Peaks laughed about it
while he was stopping
the blood.

MISS FLORENCE JACKSON

Mother said thirty years ago
Miss Jackson had been a handsome
soft-haired girl getting
her certificate from Radford
and coming back home
to teach high-school math.
But I had trouble seeing back
past that loose flesh
that flapped on her arm
when she wrote staccato
on the blackboard.
They moved the high school
20 miles away to the county seat,
but she stayed there
taught sixth grade
like a kind of basic training,
and got the boys
to make her new paddles
every time she broke an old one.
James Newman,
drawing pictures of her,
called her "old goose bosom,"
and Bernard Burchett said
she had a voice
like a good sharp hatchet.
Grimmer than God one morning
she told us there would be no more
wrestling matches
between the boys and the girls
during recess,
and that put a permanent
stop to it.

In class I told a joke
my grandaddy had told Peaks
and I hadn't understood
about a cow and a bull
and a preacher,
and she sent me to Mr. Whitt's office.
He made me go back
and tell her I was sorry,
to which she replied
she was too.
Angry in Geography she told
us the explanation for birth control:
"People have a choice
about whether or not
to have children."
They say Miss Jackson
mellowed out
just before she died,
but I was always afraid of her,
everybody was.

JEEP ALLEY, EMPEROR OF BASEBALL

Jeep stayed a senior
3 years to pitch ball
because Mr. Whitt was
coach and principal,
but the baseball team
disappeared along with
the high school, and Jeep
was left stranded, just
hanging around the diamond
in warm weather waiting
for us sixth and seventh grade
boys to come play a pick-
up game, cussing us out
for missing grounders or
dropping easy pop-ups.
It flattered us he was
interested because Jeep
weighed better than 200
pounds, always wore his old
blue Yankee cap, and could
fire without even trying
a fastball none of us could
catch. Miss Jackson tried
running him off, but Jeep
treated her like he would
a little thunder shower
that had to be politely
waited out, and we lied for
him because baseball was
the only game any of us
knew how to play, and God
it was good to hear him holler,

"Christ Almighty, Burchett, getcha glove down ina dirt and keepya god damn eyes ona ball."

JANIE SWECKER AND ME
AND GONE WITH THE WIND

Janie Swecker had to act
like she wasn't half
as smart as she was
because if she rattled off
the facts fast as she could
think of them, Miss Jackson
would sniff and say, "Well,
Janie, if you're that bored
with the history of your state,
why don't you go back
in the corner and sit
by yourself?" and Janie
hated that because back
there she couldn't get by
with sneaking to read those
library books she loved
while Miss Jackson drilled
the rest of us. So she made
herself talk slow and give
a wrong answer now and then,
and we stopped teasing her
after we understood that
if we hadn't got it done
she'd do our homework
for us even though she did
C. H. King's and Leo Spraker's
on a regular basis. Janie
let me borrow her mother's
copy of Gone with the Wind,

got impatient with me
to finish it but finally
I did and after that in class
sometimes we'd look at each
other and know what we knew.
One night I even dreamed
Miss Jackson was marching
through Georgia,
Atlanta was burning,
and I was riding hard
to pull Janie
out of the flames.

MY BROTHER, BEAUTIFUL SHINAULT, THAT GOAT

My brother and I
always got burnt
in any kind of trade
like once I gave
Gilmer Hyatt half
a stamp collection
for two hamsters,
one fell out
of my pocket
on my way home,
the other one died
two days later,
but the worst was
Beautiful Shinault
getting that year-
old bicycle
off my brother
for a rusted-out
wagon and a goat
that was two-thirds
crazy, which one
day got loose
in the house
and busted up
a chair, five
dinner plates,
a window pane,
two canning jars,
and a screen door,
and after that
Mother said check
with her next
time we got to
feeling commercial-
minded.

BILL SPRAKER'S STORE, OR THE DAY
GERONIMO COULDN'T FIND THE SCOOP

It took some courage just
to walk in there where
it smelled like last year's
potatoes in the cellar,
no windows and only one
45-watt light bulb,
and Bill'd run you out fast
if you didn't say what you wanted
and pay for it right away.
And after that movie showed
up at the Fries Drive-In,.
they started calling Bill
Geronimo because he'd killed
Frenchie Paris one night
with a 20-gauge shotgun,
got acquitted on self-defense
(even though Frenchie
didn't have but one arm),
came home nervous,
with his red hair getting kinkier
and his paleface wife
and daughters getting fatter
and sleepier by the minute,
and Bill had to stop
selling ice-cream after they started
spreading that lie around town,
about how Geronimo
couldn't find the scoop one day
and so spit tobacco juice on his hand,
reached in and got a gob
and served up the cone
anyway.

WHAT HAPPENED WHEN FAY BUSHEY WOULDN'T PAY UP

Pete Bushey,
Fay's oldest illegitimate son,
had been in third grade with me,
so I knew it was hopeless
to try and collect that money
from Fay.
But Mr. Waldron,
the District Man,
in his suit and tie,
was sure he could get it out of her,
told me to wait in his car
while he went inside to talk to her.
Fay was a little brittle woman
with a rag always tied over her head
and 2 or 3 naked younguns
squalling out in the yard,
and it used to be a kind
of guessing game in town
to try to figure out who
was the father to which one,
but Fay had a temper
and a tongue to go with it,
and I wasn't surprised to see
him come scooting out the door,
holding on to his hat
like he was in a strong wind,
Fay behind him, giving him
just a medium cussing out
because he was a city man
and she wanted to be polite.

I didn't get the money,
and Fay, she lived
to be an old lady, getting a newspaper
to read just about every day of her life.
Pete offered to fight me one day
in front of the Pentecostal church,
but I declined
seeing as how it was pocket knives
he wanted to do it with.

PHOENIX HILL AND
BILL DALTON'S DADDY

Phoenix Hill got out
of prison, and Grandmama
took to keeping a pistol
on her bedside table.
I never saw him except
in my mind where it was
dark and he was crazy-
looking, had hot coals
in his head instead
of eyeballs, but Bill
Dalton at school started
telling me about Phoenix
helping his daddy work
the lumber mill up on
the mountain and how
they went in together
making whiskey up there
in a secret place nobody'd
ever find unless they knew
where it was already. Bill
got called home one day
for an emergency, and
everybody said Phoenix
had killed his daddy
with an ax, but Bill
came back next week
and straightened us out:
they'd argued about money,
Mr. Dalton had made
the mistake of turning
his back, Phoenix lifting
the ax and letting it fall;

the blade had come straight
down the middle of Bill's
daddy's skull there where
the brain is split into
two halves, and neither
half had been hurt too bad,
though he'd be laid up
for a good long time,
and nobody ever saw
Phoenix again.

WHAT PIG CLEMONS TOLD MY MOTHER

She saw him
hunkered down
by the store
over at Porter's Crossroads.
His mouth was gaped open
like it usually was,
and he was staring out
into space with one arm
kind of gangled out
in front of him
like maybe he wanted
a ride but maybe he didn't.
So she stopped the car
— he'd gone to school
with my brother —
and Pig climbed in,
looking gloomy
but polite nevertheless.
My mother,
ever the bright one,
ever the cheerful,
asked him,
"Raymond, where are you going?"
and Pig,
he looked out the window,
away from her,
and told her,
"Aw, Miss Frances,
I'm going to Wytheville
to get drunk,
and God, don't I
dread it."

WHAT HAPPENED WHEN I TRIED TO TELL DEETUM DUNFORD ABOUT NEW RIVER

He'd been AWOL
from the army
about 6 months
hiding out back
in the mountain
near Billsby, and
he was squatting
down there by
the railroad track
waiting for me
to get through
telling him about
the river. "Deetum,"
I said, "this river
flows north through
West Virginia and
joins up with the
Ohio and from there
on out into the
Mississippi and
then down south
to New Orleans.
"Deetum," I said,
"this water here is
on its way to the
Gulf of Mexico."
I stopped. He
stood up, said,
"Yep, I reckon
that's right,"
and headed up
the tracks back

on up toward the
mountain, pausing
just once to look
over his shoulder
and holler at me,
"You tell Miss
Frances I'm going
to bring her some
blackberries when
they get ripe."

MRS. GREEN

At the screen door
a pretty woman just
married and in shorts
on a Saturday in May,
she was sweet to me
when I came up to collect,
offered me something cold
to drink,
            which I refused
for the sake of dreaming
the whole summer I was
twelve about what it
would be like some
morning to walk
softly into
that lady's
kitchen.

SHOOTING CROWS

Mostly it was starlings
and grackles that landed in
those trees of an evening,
but we called them crows,
and I'd sit out there on
the side of Broomsage Hill,
waiting for Grandad to take
a shot at them, which he
would do two or three times
before it got dark. Now
and then he'd hit one, I'd
watch it fall, tear off over
there under the tree to try
to get a look, once grandly
horrified to see it flapping
spattering red splotches on
the milkweed leaves, and I
couldn't understand why he
never wanted to see a dead
one, didn't even try all that
hard to hit one, would just
sit sit there in his khaki work
clothes and smoke one Camel
after another and spit now
and then, try to tease me
about that red-headed Delby
girl I wasn't even slightly
interested in. I liked how
it smelled, though, after he
shot and he'd let me chamber
the fat shells for him. And

once he even let me have a
sip of what he was drinking
though he cautioned me twice
not to let the old battle ax,
by which he meant my grandmama,
find out about it.

MY GRANDADDY
MOSTLY WITH HIS KNIFE

Balanced a row of peas on it
all the way up to his mouth;
poured coffee cup to saucer
and back until it got cool;
sat back smoking and told us
how at mealtime Uncle Dave
and his daddy had had terrible
arguments about that war
the one had fought in
and the other hadn't,
how Uncle Bill threw a cat
in a crock of liver pudding,
how he'd fired a train
back and forth between Roanoke
and Charleston, West Virginia;
had a pocket watch he'd check
every time he heard a whistle;
drank pretty heavy of an evening
and promised to take me with him
to Bristol to buy me a gold
cornet but never got around to it;
sat after dark in the study,
Grandmama behind him listening
to Lowell Thomas with her eyes
shut and nodding her head;
wrote stuff on the backs
of old envelopes: chemical formulae,
algebra problems, names of hotels;
said he was just trying
to remember what he'd forgotten;

told me to go practice my music;
tried to whistle for me
even though he was tone deaf
the only tune he ever much liked:
There'll Be a Hot Time
in the Old Town
Tonight.

MONKEY, DUDE, HAT, AND HITLER

Monkey Dunford didn't take a paper
because first of all he'd have had
to get his wife to read it to him
and secondly he was Church of God
and prayed out loud in Grandad's barn
every day at lunchtime,
but Dude took one even though they said
it took him all day to read it,
and Hat took one too.
She was their baby sister,
had one of those sanctimonious
Pentecostal faces,
and spent most of her time
down at Price's store telling people
what the paper said that morning.
Now Hitler, he took one only
on Sunday because he said he liked to read
the funny papers, but everybody knew
he did it just to get Monkey's goat,
and I'd seen him myself, threshing wheat
one day, catch a black snake
close to five feet long,
chase Monkey all over the field with it,
and then demonstrate for us
how you could snap its head off
by catching hold of its tail
and cracking that thing like a whip.
I had to laugh every time
I threw one on Hitler's porch,

thinking about that tale Grandad
made up about Hitler getting mad
at his old lady, getting down his shotgun
and trying to shoot her
but then having to beat hell out of her
because she'd ducked out of his sights
and caused him to ruin
their new refrigerator.

THRESHING WHEAT

My job was to hold the bags
at the end of the chute,
grain sometimes coming down
fast and thick as water.
I grunted to lift those bags,
and Crow Jim'd spit and cuss
me out if I slipped and let
any wheat spill on the ground.
I liked to chew that stuff,
making something somewhere between
chewing gum and bread in my mouth.
One day up in Jim Early's field,
we saw a buck deer, antlers big
as rocking chairs, being chased
by dogs, come out of the woods,
stand still there a minute looking
at the trucks, the tractor, that
house-sized threshing machine,
the men with pitchforks and one
boy scuttering all around.
Then slow as in a dream it
jumped the fence and loped easy
down the hill, the dogs still
yapping back up in the woods.
We all stopped work and hollered
until Peaks told us to get off
our asses and start earning our pay.
In the back of the pick-up going
home, we talked about that deer:

Crow Jim swore if he'd had a gun
he'd have shot it, Hitler saying
he'd seen plenty bigger, and Monkey
patting that New Testament he kept
in his top overalls pocket, pulling
me over so close beside him I could
smell the sweat and whispering it
was a sign sent down by God.

CARBIDE PLANT

They hauled the dust and waste out
and dumped it in a field,
2 or 3 acres splotched with gray
piles of stuff that was dangerous
because when it gets wet
carbide makes a gas that burns.
In the rain one time
Frank Sawyers and somebody else
drove a truck out there
and found themselves all of a sudden
surrounded by fire.
The other man ran,
but Frank decided to crawl
under the truck, and of course
the tires burst from the heat.
He was caught under that truck
for 5 or 6 hours, burnt all to hell
but not dead even though he
and my father and the men
who worked at getting him out
wished he was.
My father couldn't eat or sleep,
said he couldn't help
but smell it.
After about a year, Frank
got out of the hospital.
Later on, my father
got to be works manager
until New York closed the plant down
and sent him to Louisville,

where he did his work all right
but got severe shortness
of breath and psoriasis
and asked to be sent home.
Out there he was even shot at
by some of the union men on strike,
but he said things like that
can happen anywhere.

EVENING SERVICES
EVERY FOURTH SUNDAY

Dr. Gwathmey came
20 miles
for Mrs. Frye
and just 2 families.
It was funny
Grandmama was
almost too little
to pump anything
on that old organ
except Now the Day
Is Over, with
her glasses slid down
to the tip of her nose
and her mouth all
pursed up tight.
Grandad sat in back,
wouldn't stand
or kneel or pray
or sing but always
too late said Amen
because he'd built
that chapel, then
(for spite Grandmama
said) painted it
his favorite color:
yellow. I had a blue
shirt and wore it
for Toots Pope.

She had black hair
and sometimes stood
beside me outside
in the dark. After
vespers our parents
talked in soft
murmurs, the air
full of cricket
and frog noises,
summer wind,
the smell of
rain coming
later.

WHAT FINALLY HAPPENED
TO PETE BUSHEY

Usually he'd be out in the yard
where I had to walk past
to get to Mrs. McGavock's
piano lesson,
and Pete'd holler at me
and maybe throw a rock or two
if he thought about it,
Fay yelling at him from inside the house
to leave me alone.
Pete got bitter
failing fifth grade 3 years in a row,
reached the legal age to quit school,
and took to playing poker
down by the river
or up behind the ball diamond
or over at Vivien Sexton's house,
and then later on he got caught
breaking into Price's store,
did a little time
working for the governor,
and came home even less cheerful
than he had been.
Drunk one hot afternoon,
he stood outside Billy Mabe's house
and called him every kind of a son of a bitch
until Billy finally ran him off
with an ax.
Otis Shannon told me about it
in the barber shop a few months later
when I was home from college,
how Pete went home to get his knife,

went back out
and caught Billy in the alley,
chased him a ways down the dirt path
there behind the hardware store,
jumped on Billy's back
rode him a little ways,
hollering like a crazy man,
and finally cut his throat.
Otis said Pete stood
and watched awhile,
then walked on back home
to wait for the deputy
to come and get him.
Otis and I agreed,
while he was slapping witch hazel
on the back of my neck,
that what Pete did
was a god damn dirty rotten shame.

MY BROTHER FLIES OVER LOW

Nobody could believe
my brother ever got through
that pilot school in Texas
because it was well known
in town he couldn't drive
a car worth a damn. So he'd
made a point of wearing his
uniform whenever he came
home and telling people
to watch out for him, he
was going to fly over low
one of these days. Which
he did, he and a buddy also
stationed down in Goldsboro,
made 2 passes, each one sounding
like 14 freight trains
falling off a cliff, waggled
their wings and headed on back
down to North Carolina,
gaining altitude as they went.
Mother was hanging out a wash,
and Mary King was coming up
the hill to help her with
spring cleaning, and they say
Miss Ossie Price came running
out of her store to see what
was the matter. And nobody
sees my brother now but what
they grin at him, shake their
heads and say something like,
"Great God Almighty, Bill."

Mother won't talk about it
in public, claims to be
embarrassed about the whole
thing, but she doesn't fool
anybody.

AUNT INEZ AND
THE OLD LAWSON PLACE

My father spoke to the town men
who sat every day on the steps.
We walked by them
up the hill to the back porch,
the path through the honeysuckled yard,
to see Aunt Inez
with her matchstick arms,
her skin too pale,
and her hacked-off hair, gray as tin.
He took off his hat
and asked how she was.
She said, her voice muffled and low,
I'm fine, Richard, how are you?
He told her what food we'd brought.
She thanked him, said she didn't need it.
He said she should eat more.
She said yes, he was right.
He pumped her a bucket of water,
she thanked him,
and we went down the hill again,
me looking back just once
to see her sitting at the kitchen window,
her back turned toward town,
and her horse's eyes watching me.
My father spoke to the town men,
and they spoke back.

Inez was the baby of the Lawson family,
had been good at calligraphy,
astrology, fixing watches,
and auto mechanics,

had once when I was little
and full of teasing
slapped me off Grandmama's back porch.
When she died
great nieces and nephews
came to scavenge from miles away.
Then the house and what was left
was auctioned off.
Aunt Inez's 1928 Chevrolet,
locked up where she'd parked it
one morning thirty years ago,
went for sixteen hundred dollars.

GOING, 1960–1970

1.

My roommate in Charlottesville
was from Youngstown, Ohio,
a doctor's son, whose parents
took us to Farmington Country
Club and drove me home once
in a Cadillac, first one
except Barnett's hearse
that'd ever been
in our driveway.

2.

First airplane
I ever rode was south
to Fort Jackson, South Carolina,
for basic training, but a train
took me north again
to Baltimore, and I was used
to that.

3.

Monika Litskus
was a Polish girl I danced with
in Stuttgart bars, and hell,
we might have gotten married
if I'd have known
a language to ask
her in.

4.

I took a ferry
from Landau, Denmark,
to Göteborg, Sweden, and there
was tax-free liquor on board
that got all those crazy Swedes
mean drunk and fighting,
and even though that
was on the North Sea
it reminded me
of home.

5.

I spent a Thanksgiving
in Luxembourg City, but it
was raining, so I didn't see
much except a skinned rabbit
and a deer carcass hanging outside
somebody's butcher shop,
and they'd written me
from home that
my grandfather
was sick.

6.

I surprised Mother
while she was ironing,
hadn't told anybody I was coming
home on my way west of Hawaii,
wore my khakis and spitshined
boots over to see Grandad.
He had his shirt off, trying
to shave sitting down
in front of a mirror.
He'd cut himself
3 or 4 times he was
shaking so bad.

7.

Helicopters
flew me in
to an old, cracked
French-built tennis court
near the capital city of
Binh Chanh Province
so that one Asian
could beat up
another one
under my
super-
vision.

8.

Drunk on a back street
in Tokyo well after midnight
I was cussed out in perfect English
for something I was only partially
aware of being guilty of by
the most beautiful whore
I'd ever seen.

9.

Marines told me
some things they'd done
but in Bangkok I didn't want
to start trading that kind of stories
because, Christ, for eleven dollars
you could spend a night
and a day with a woman
you'd dream about years
later.

10.

I had a plan
for when I was discharged
of spending the night in the best
hotel San Francisco had to offer
and laying down $100 for some
good-smelling California girl,
but funny thing was I went
straight to the airport
and caught the first
flight home.

11.

He was still alive
though they'd kept him off
whiskey all that time, and he
was delighted I'd drive him to
the Wytheville liquor store where
they spoke to him by name and he bought
five fifths of I. W. Harper, had me carry
the package and hide it in the car trunk,
but even though we met her at the door
and lied we'd been to the optometrist's,
Grandmama found those bottles
before he even got a sip,
went out and on rocks
behind the garage
broke every
god damn
one.

12.

In white tie
and tails my father
danced the first two
times in his life, first
with my bride and then with
her mother. There were close
to 300 people watching, and he
kept a smile on his face, got
through it just fine. I felt
like kissing him because I'd
been through enough of a
war to know courage
when I saw it.

13.

I was up there
going to Columbia
and drinking cocktails
with writers who knew my name,
but when Mother called
that morning and gave me the news,
he'd got up around five,
gone in to pee,
died standing there
(not a joke! not a joke!),
fell wedging his head
between the bathtub and the wall,
my father working
almost an hour getting him out,
knowing all that time
his father was gone,
the only thing I could think
was I have to
get a haircut,
I have to
drive down there,
I have to
go down.

14.

It was sunny and cold,
but I didn't feel anything,
I was like something cut
out of a sheet of tin,
and then I saw my father
take off his glasses,
doing what I'd never
in 30 years seen him do,
and swab at his eyes,
and I felt a hurt snap
through my whole body,
wanted just for that instant
to plunge down with him
into that grave, going down
into black dirt, keep going
down with him the rest
of my life.

GIFTS

Plenty of men
already in this family
was Mother's verdict
over news our child
was a daughter.
My father was happy enough
to see that girl baby,
having wondered out loud
several years when we'd get
around to what he called
the main business
of raising children.
He and I talked
about the house
I'd just bought,
or as he put it,
the mortgage I'd signed,
and while my wife
and mother and daughter
were busy doing whatever
it is that two women
and a baby do
upstairs in a bedroom,
he and I went over
across the field to get
some things from Grandad's
old tool shop.
No woman
had ever much cared
for that place
while he was alive,

and the right smells
were still there inside,
the right lack of light,
but the old man's clutter
had been replaced
by an orderliness
he would have found
horrifying.
I looked for the glass
with the dancing girls
who took off their clothes
when you filled it
with water or whiskey,
the naked woman
paperweight,
but they were gone,
and I was outraged
into discoursing
on why the hell
anybody would live
in a place where
people stole
anything of value,
the human condition
was unbearable
enough, even in
civilized towns,
but my father
only half listened
and opened up
a cabinet for me
to get what I'd need.

I took down a wrench,
a saw, some wire pliers,
a couple of screwdrivers.
He picked out
the oldest hammer there,
offered it to me,
and I took it
from his hand.

PITT POETRY SERIES

Ed Ochester, General Editor